NFL
TODAY

THE STORY OF THE
TENNESSEE TITANS

NFL TODAY

THE STORY OF THE TENNESSEE TITANS

LORI DITTMER

CREATIVE EDUCATION

Cover: Houston Oilers defense, 1996 (top), running
back LenDale White (bottom)
Page 2: Titans defense, 2007
Pages 4–5: Quarterback Vince Young
Pages 6–7: Titans offensive linemen, 2007

. . . .

Published by Creative Education
P.O. Box 227, Mankato, Minnesota 56002
Creative Education is an imprint of
The Creative Company
www.thecreativecompany.us

Design and production by Blue Design
Design Associate: Sarah Yakawonis
Printed in the United States of America

Photographs by Corbis (Bettmann), Getty Images
(Brian Bahr, Scott Boehm, Gary Bogdon/Sports
Illustrated, Jonathan Daniel, Jonathan Daniel/
Allsport, Jerome Davis/NFL, Diamond Images,
Tony Duffy/Allsport, Stephen Dunn, Chad Ehlers,
George Gojkovich, Paul Jasienski, Allen Kee/NFL,
Al Messerschmidt, Al Messerschmidt/NFL, Doug
Pensinger, Mark Perlstein//Time & Life Pictures,
Paul Spinelli, Rick Stewart/Allsport, Rick Stewart,
Matthew Stockman, George Tiedemann/Sports
Illustrated, Lou Witt/NFL, Michael Zagaris)

Library of Congress Cataloging-in-Publication Data

Dittmer, Lori.
The story of the Tennessee Titans / by Lori Dittmer.
p. cm. — (NFL today)
Includes index.
ISBN 978-1-58341-773-7
1. Tennessee Titans (Football team)—History—
Juvenile literature. I. Title. II. Series.

GV956.T45D57 2009
796.332'640976855—dc22   2008022707

First Edition
9 8 7 6 5 4 3 2 1

CONTENTS

ON THE SIDELINES

MEET THE OILERS/TITANS

A START AT THE TOP

X--

X Nashville
continued to grow
as a major American
city by obtaining two
big-league sports
franchises in the late
1990s: football's Titans,
in 1997, and hockey's
Predators, in 1998.

Music and the state of Tennessee go hand in hand. Known as the birthplace of country and blues music, Tennessee produced the first commercial FM radio station and is home to the *Grand Ole Opry*, America's longest-running radio show. With many recording studios in Nashville, the state's capital, Tennessee has become a stomping ground for musical artists of all genres. This history has earned Nashville the nickname "Music City."

In its earlier days, Nashville was sometimes referred to as the "Athens of the South." One of the more refined and educated Southern cities of the mid-1800s, Nashville was the first Southern city to establish a public school system. While embracing the Athenian ideals of education and innovation, Nashville also incorporated classical Greek styles into some of its buildings. Even today, Nashville boasts the Parthenon, a replica of the original building from ancient Athens, Greece. It's fitting, therefore, that Tennessee's professional football team, the Titans of the National Football League (NFL), would look to Greek mythology for its name.

The Titans franchise started out not on the bluegrass hills of Tennessee, but on the dusty plains of Texas. In 1959, a wealthy oil businessman named K. S. "Bud" Adams joined forces with owners in seven other cities who wanted to compete in professional football. Together, they formed a new league called the American Football League (AFL), and Adams named his team the Oilers, after the natural resource so plentiful in Texas.

At first, most AFL players were either old NFL players or those who had played in college but went undrafted. With head coach Lou Rymkus at the helm, the Oilers signed running back Billy Cannon, who had just won the Heisman Trophy as the best player in college football. However, Cannon had also signed a $50,000-a-year contract with the Los Angeles Rams. The Oilers offered him twice as much. The NFL challenged the contract in court, and the Oilers won, which boosted the AFL's credibility as a professional league.

The Oilers' first roster also featured George Blanda, a quarterback who had played with the Chicago Bears for 10 seasons. While many football observers thought the veteran was washed up, Blanda would prove his worth by throwing 24 touchdown passes in the Oilers' first season, mostly to receivers Charley Hennigan and Bill Groman. Blanda would

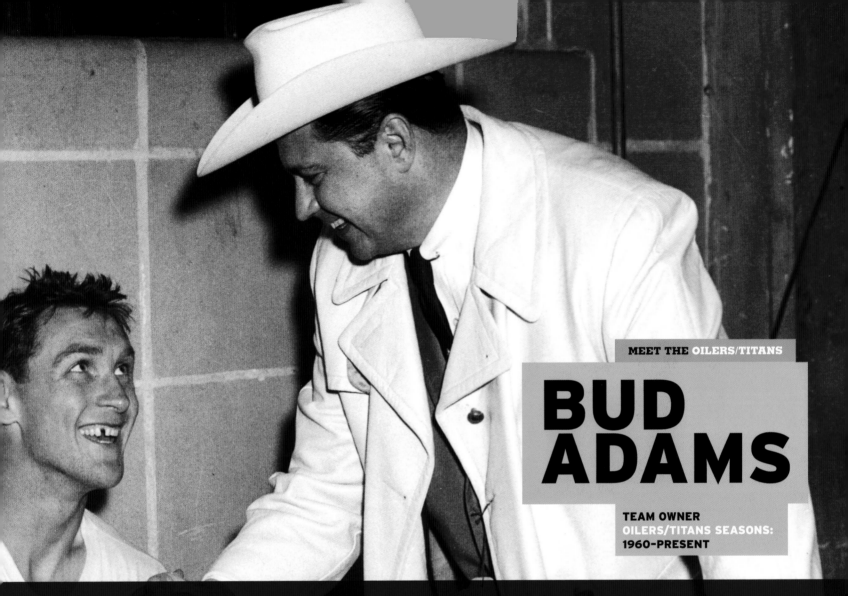

BUD ADAMS

TEAM OWNER
OILERS/TITANS SEASONS:
1960-PRESENT

From the Oilers' beginnings in Houston to the Titans' Tennessee home today, K. S. "Bud" Adams Jr. has been in the owner's seat, guiding his franchise every step of the way. After Adams started the ADA Oil Company in 1946, the wealthy Texas businessman sponsored amateur teams in basketball and softball and held ownership in professional basketball, baseball, and boxing. In 1959, Adams wanted to join the NFL with a team in Houston, but the NFL turned him down. So he helped to create the AFL, which rivaled the NFL for a decade before the NFL absorbed the AFL in 1970. Adams began searching for a new stadium for the Oilers as early as 1987, when he publicly talked to Jacksonville, Florida, about a possible relocation. Eight years later, Nashville, Tennessee, agreed to build a stadium for the team, and Adams announced that the Oilers would move for the 1997 season. Although he spent big bucks on his Titans, he also believed in giving back to the community. By 2008, local Tennessee charities had received roughly $16 million as a result of Adams's charitable work.

ON THE SIDELINES

DOUBLE OVERTIME IN TEXAS

Nearly 38,000 fans packed Houston's Jeppesen Stadium in December 1962 to watch a championship battle between the AFL's two Texas teams, the Oilers and the Dallas Texans. For the Texans, the championship was their last game representing Dallas. They were planning on moving to Kansas City, Missouri, where they would become the Chiefs. The Oilers, meanwhile, were hoping to claim their third straight AFL championship. At halftime, the Texans led 17–0, but the Oilers staged a comeback—which included a George Blanda touchdown pass and field goal, followed by a touchdown run by running back Charlie Tolar—to tie the game with less than six minutes on the clock. The Oilers had a chance at a game-winning field goal in the last seconds of regulation, but the Texans blocked it, sending the game into overtime. With no score after 15 minutes, the teams headed into a second overtime. This time, the Texans drove into field-goal range and ended the game with a 25-yard kick. The 20–17 Dallas win came after 78 minutes of play, making it one of the longest games in professional football history.

also double as the team's kicker, making 15 field goals and 46 points after touchdowns. Joining Cannon and Blanda in Houston's backfield was running back Charlie Tolar, who was nicknamed the "Human Bowling Ball." At just 5-foot-6, Tolar had a knack for charging underneath taller defenders.

In their debut season, the Oilers went 10–4 and won the AFL's Eastern Division championship. They then went on to play the Los Angeles Chargers in the AFL Championship Game. Houston hosted 32,000 fans for the game at Jeppesen Stadium, a renovated high school field that the Oilers called home. After Los Angeles grabbed an early lead with two field goals, Blanda rallied the Oilers to a 10–9 halftime lead. The veteran quarterback then tossed a swing pass to Cannon for a fourth-quarter score, and the Oilers won 24–16. Later, Blanda would look back on the 1960 Oilers and boast, "That first year, the Houston Oilers or the Los Angeles Chargers could have beaten the NFL champion [Philadelphia Eagles] in a Super Bowl."

The following year, under new coach Wally Lemm, the Oilers averaged 41 points a game over their last 9 games. Cannon led the charge with an AFL-best 948 rushing yards and 15 touchdowns. The Oilers finished the season with a 10–3–1 record and another trip to the league title game, where

they met the Chargers again. The second AFL Championship Game was heavy on defense, and the Oilers won 10–3 for their second title. Strong and speedy Oilers defensive end Don Floyd frustrated the Chargers, and an interception by Oilers defensive back Julian Spence clinched the win. "I feel like someone who inherited a million dollars in tarnished silverware," said Coach Lemm, who had taken over in midseason. "All I did was polish it."

Oilers fans were hoping for a "three-peat" in 1962 when the team won the Eastern Division for the third straight year. The Oilers faced another Texas team, the Dallas Texans, for the league championship. The Oilers tied the game in the fourth quarter when Tolar dove into the end zone for a one-yard score, and the game went into the first of two overtimes. In the end, though, Houston came up short, losing 20–17.

That loss signaled the start of a disappointing stretch for the Oilers and their fans. Age and injury began to bog the team down, and Houston dropped to 6–8 in 1963. The slide continued as the Oilers finished the next three seasons with losing records.

The Oilers finally got back above .500 in 1967 after adding such terrific players as safety Ken Houston, linebacker George Webster, and 6-foot-9 defensive tackle Ernie Ladd. Houston's

EARL CAMPBELL

RUNNING BACK
OILERS SEASONS: 1978–84
HEIGHT: 5-FOOT-11
WEIGHT: 232 POUNDS

Nicknamed the "Tyler Rose" (after his hometown of Tyler, Texas), Earl Campbell burst onto the professional football scene in 1978. The former Heisman Trophy winner was named both Rookie of the Year and the NFL's Most Valuable Player (MVP) after his debut season. Although Campbell was soft-spoken, there was nothing quiet about his playing style. He possessed great speed, incredible strength, and a powerful stiff arm, and he used them to get around—or, more often, to go *through*—opposing defenders. After Campbell's rookie season, he just got better. His huge, powerful thighs made him incredibly difficult to topple; defensive players usually had to gang-tackle him to bring him down. Despite the pounding his body took, he played in nearly every game, missing only 6 games out of 115 in Houston due to injury. During the 1980 season, Campbell rushed for more than 200 yards in 4 different games. In comparing Campbell to University of Oklahoma running back Billy Sims, who had won the Heisman Trophy the year after Campbell, Oklahoma Sooners coach Barry Switzer once said, "Earl Campbell is the greatest player that ever suited up. Billy Sims is human. Campbell isn't."

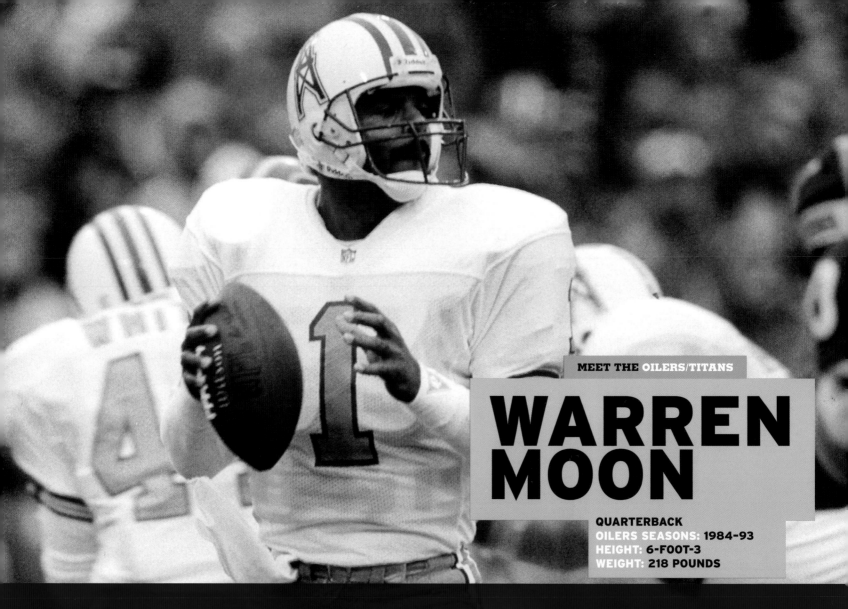

WARREN MOON

QUARTERBACK
OILERS SEASONS: 1984–93
HEIGHT: 6-FOOT-3
WEIGHT: 218 POUNDS

After finishing his college career at the University of Washington, Warren Moon was not drafted by any NFL team. Undaunted, he refused to give up his dream of being a professional football quarterback. For six years, Moon played for the Edmonton Eskimos in the Canadian Football League, where the quarterback refined his skills and led his team to five Grey Cup titles as league champion. He finally made his way to the NFL when he joined the Oilers in 1984. Initially, he struggled with accuracy; during his first three seasons in the NFL, Moon threw for 40 touchdowns and 59 interceptions. Then, in 1986, the team implemented the "run-and-shoot" offense, which showcased Moon's rocket arm and quick feet. Oilers head coach Jack Pardee once said of Moon, "he's got the height, he's got a good arm, and he studies football—he's everything we're looking for in a quarterback." Known for throwing picture-perfect spirals, Moon became the face of the franchise, leading his team to the playoffs in each of his last seven years with the Oilers. In 2006, Moon became the first African American quarterback elected to the Pro Football Hall of Fame.

power shifted to the defensive side of the ball, and the team allowed a league-low average of 14 points per game on the season. The Oilers won their division with a 9–4–1 record but were unable to capture the AFL title, losing to the Oakland Raiders in the Championship Game.

Defensive end Elvin Bethea, who displayed a frightening combination of quickness, power, and durability, joined the Oilers in 1968. During his 16 seasons with the Oilers, he would play in a franchise-record 210 games and give his all in each one. Bethea's college coach, Hornsby Howell, later explained that Bethea "was the kind of athlete who worked hard even when nobody was watching."

Despite strong performances by Blanda, Houston, and Bethea—all eventual Hall-of-Famers—the Oilers' 1967 season was the team's only winning campaign from 1963 to 1970. After the AFL and NFL merged in 1970, the Oilers continued to struggle. Dan Pastorini, a tough quarterback known for his willingness to play through pain and injury, joined Houston as the team's first pick in the 1971 NFL Draft. But playing behind a weak offensive line, Pastorini was sacked often and rendered ineffective. In both 1972 and 1973, the Oilers finished an embarrassing 1–13.

BUM AND THE EARLERS

X A native Texan known for his folksy and colorful quotes, coach Bum Phillips once said, "The Dallas Cowboys may be America's team, but the Houston Oilers are Texas's team."

The Oilers promoted defensive coordinator O. A. "Bum" Phillips to head coach in 1975, ushering in an era of increased fan support for the team. Phillips, who looked like the stereotypical Texan in his ten-gallon hat, snakeskin boots, and Western shirts, assembled a bruising defense that included Bethea and linebackers Gregg Bingham and Robert Brazile. Phillips used a "3-4" defense, with only three linemen and four linebackers—a formation that was effective at stopping the run. The defensive package, adopted from the University of Oklahoma, was just starting to spread to professional football.

On offense, Pastorini had two great passing targets: receivers Ken Burrough and Billy "White Shoes" Johnson, who had joined the Oilers in 1971 and 1974 respectively. Known for his bright white shoes and goofy end zone dances, Johnson would tie an NFL record in 1975 by returning four kicks for touchdowns. Although he stood just 5-foot-9, Johnson had a knack for darting away from his much larger opponents. "He

X Billy Johnson was originally ignored by most NFL teams due to his small size; the Oilers didn't select him until the 15th round of the 1974 NFL Draft.

was even more exciting in practice," Phillips said later. "We didn't have anyone who could tackle him."

Although the Oilers missed the playoffs in 1975, they went a solid 10–4 and had fans flocking to the Houston Astrodome. The fans' enthusiasm led to "Luv Ya Blue"—a movement in the late '70s that involved special cheers and a theme song about the players and their Columbia blue uniforms. The team song, "Luv Ya Blue," is one of the best-remembered in NFL history.

Plagued by injuries, the Oilers went just 5–9 and 8–6 the next two seasons. But in 1978, Houston emerged as a powerhouse. That year, the Oilers identified Earl Campbell, a 230-pound running back, as the best player available in the NFL Draft. Unfortunately, the Oilers were scheduled to pick 17th in the Draft. Phillips negotiated with the Tampa Bay Buccaneers, offering them three draft picks, a third-round

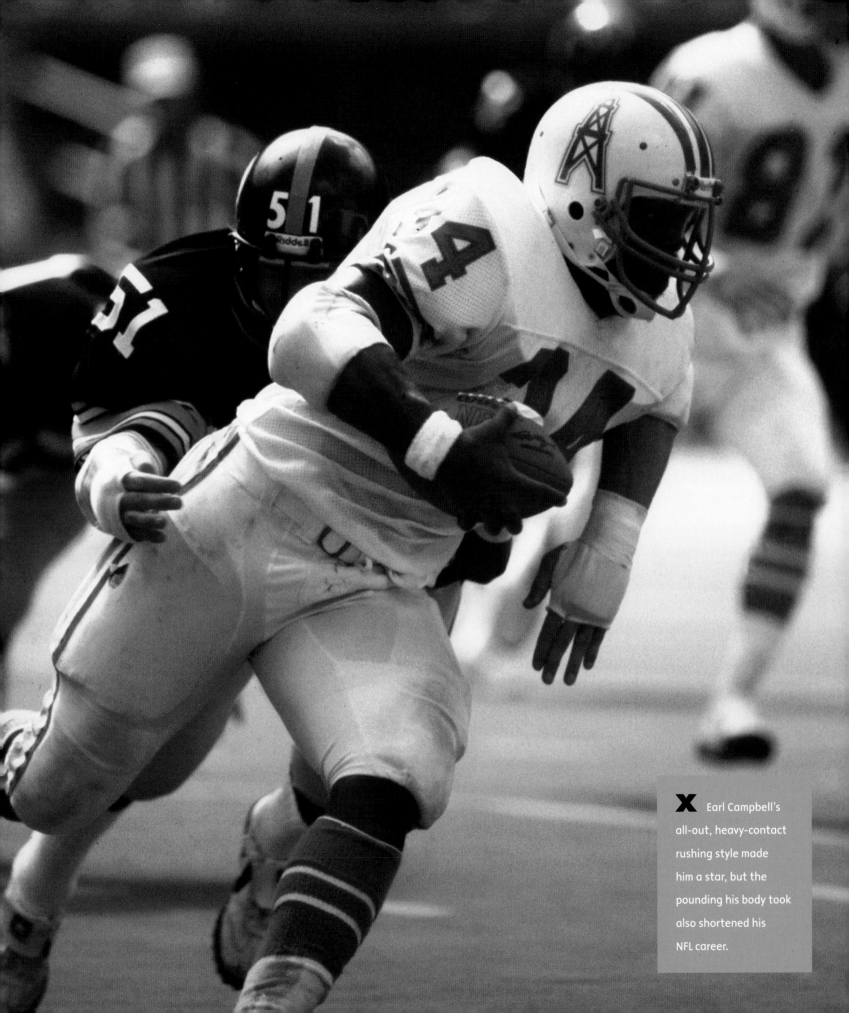

X Earl Campbell's all-out, heavy-contact rushing style made him a star, but the pounding his body took also shortened his NFL career.

ON THE SIDELINES

FROM ROUGHNECK TO T-RAC

During the Oilers' 37 seasons in Houston, their name and logo reflected the economy of the region, as many of Texas's cities and much of the industry in the state is based on oil. The Oilers wore helmets with an oil derrick logo, and their mascot was a "roughneck," or oil field worker. When the Oilers moved to Tennessee, those monikers no longer fit, and the NFL retired the Oilers name so that no other team could use it. In 1999, the Tennessee franchise took the name Titans, but it wasn't the first professional football team to use the name. New York's AFL team began as the Titans before becoming the Jets in 1963. In Greek mythology, the Titans were a race of giant gods. As part of the myth, one of the Titans, Prometheus, gave fire to humans. For the Tennessee Titans, the name was meant to reflect strong, heroic qualities. Along with the new Titans name, the team introduced a new fireball logo. Owner Bud Adams also selected the team's new mascot. Named T-Rac, the mascot is a raccoon, the official state wild animal of Tennessee.

choice the following year, and Oilers tight end Jimmie Giles. In return, Houston was able to draft the bruising running back known as the "Tyler Rose." A nationally televised Monday Night Football game against the Miami Dolphins that season let the Oilers showcase their new star, as Campbell rushed over and through defenders for 199 yards and 4 touchdowns. Fans began to call the Oilers the "Earlers."

With a 10–6 record, the Oilers finally reached the playoffs in 1978. They eked out a win over the Dolphins and then sailed past the New England Patriots, setting up a showdown with the Steelers in Pittsburgh for the American Football Conference (AFC) championship. Playing on an icy field and facing Pittsburgh's famous "Steel Curtain" defense, the Oilers committed nine turnovers and lost 34–5. Afterwards, the Oilers returned to the Astrodome, where about 50,000 vocal fans were waiting to show their support. "This is the beginning of 1979 for us," said receiver Mike Barber.

In 1979, the Oilers suffered another loss, this time 27–13, to Pittsburgh in a rematch for the AFC championship. The next year, the Oakland Raiders bounced Houston from the playoffs in the first round. Frustrated by the playoff failures, Bud Adams then fired Phillips as head coach.

ANOTHER TRY AT A TITLE

By the early 1980s, most of the Oilers' stars had retired or moved on to other teams; Campbell, the brightest star, would be traded to the New Orleans Saints in 1984 for a first-round draft pick. Houston lacked solid leadership and went through several coaches, including Ed Biles, Chuck Studley, and Hugh Campbell. The Oilers became known as one of the worst teams in the NFL, wrapping up their 1983 season at just 2–14.

Houston's decline began to turn around with the 1984 acquisition of quarterback Warren Moon, a former Canadian Football League standout. After joining the Oilers, Moon began firing passes to the talented receiving trio of Drew Hill, Ernest Givins, and Haywood Jeffires. He completed his first NFL season with 3,338 passing yards, breaking George Blanda's 1961 team record.

Late in the 1985 season, defensive coordinator Jerry Glanville was promoted to head coach. Glanville, known for his black attire and sharp wit, said his goal was to turn the Astrodome into a "House of Pain" for opponents—to make his

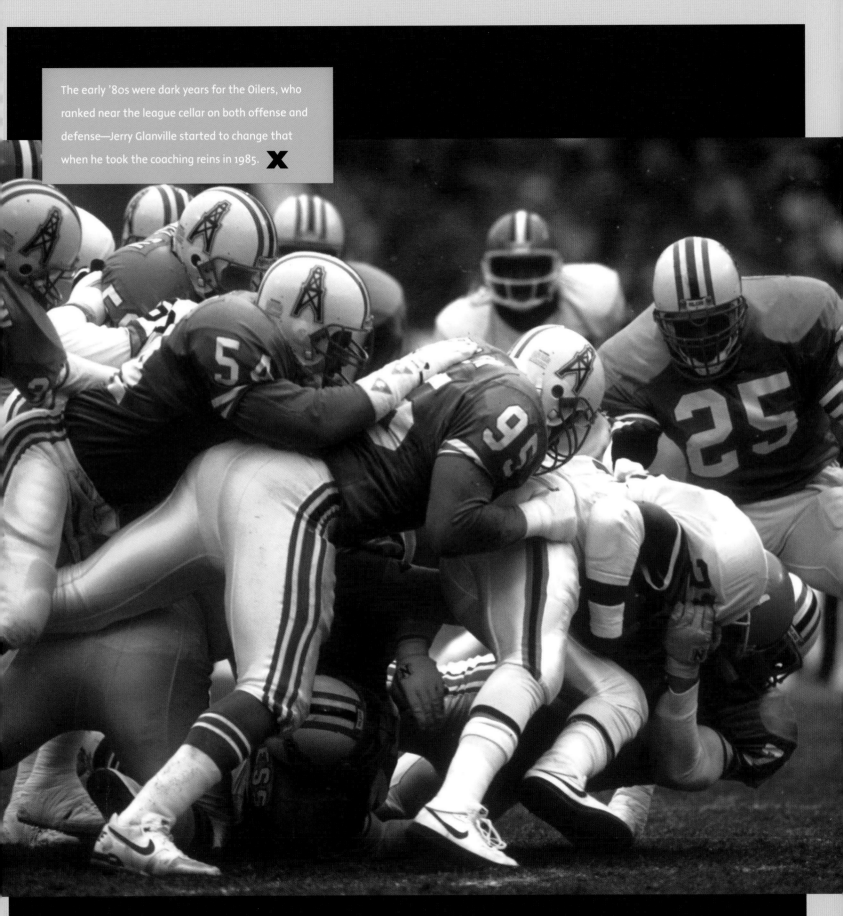

The early '80s were dark years for the Oilers, who ranked near the league cellar on both offense and defense—Jerry Glanville started to change that when he took the coaching reins in 1985. **X**

ON THE SIDELINES

THE RUN-AND-SHOOT

The "run-and-shoot" offense originated in the 1970s, but the pass-heavy strategy did not really make its way into professional football playbooks until the 1980s. Oilers quarterbacks coach June Jones began using some of the run-and-shoot's concepts in 1987. When Jack Pardee took over as head coach in 1990, the Oilers went to a full-time run-and-shoot offense, in which quarterback Warren Moon (pictured) would roll toward the sidelines and fire passes to receivers racing across or down the field. From 1990 to 1992, the Oilers led the NFL in passing yards, averaging 4,485 per season. However, with only one running back, four wide receivers, and no tight ends on the field, the strategy earned a reputation for being risky. Without a tight end or second running back to help the offensive line, the quarterback often was left vulnerable to blitzing defenders. By 1994, the Oilers moved away from the run-and-shoot, and opposing defenders rejoiced. "Tell the owner thank you and tell the front office thank you," said Pittsburgh Steelers cornerback Rod Woodson. "I think defenses all over the league are going to be very relieved."

team more aggressive and intimidating. "When I came here in '84, we had the nicest guys in the NFL," Glanville later said. "But they couldn't hit if you handed them sticks."

Glanville fortified his defense with swift cornerback Cris Dishman and linemen Ray Childress and William Fuller, while offensive lineman Bruce Matthews—who had joined the Oilers in 1983—helped stabilize the offense. Glanville built his offense around Moon, who quickly became a fan favorite akin to Earl Campbell. Fans flocked to the Astrodome, and the Oilers did not disappoint them. Houston finished 9–6 in 1987 and made the playoffs for the first of seven straight seasons.

Although Houston consistently made the postseason, the team fell short of the Super Bowl every time. After the 1989 season, Glanville was replaced by former NFL linebacker Jack Pardee. To take advantage of Moon's strong arm and scrambling ability, Coach Pardee installed the "run-and-shoot" offense, and Moon thrived in it. In a December 1990 road game against the Kansas City Chiefs, Moon passed for 527 yards, the second-highest total in NFL history. In both the 1990 and 1991 seasons, Moon threw for nearly 4,700 yards. Catching most of his tosses were Jeffires and Hill. In 1991, the pair accumulated the most receptions (190) ever by two teammates in one season.

X Although 1992 ended with a wrenching playoff loss for the Oilers, it was the greatest season of halfback Lorenzo White's career, as he ran for 1,226 yards and made the Pro Bowl.

Unfortunately, the Oilers' playoff woes continued. The most heartbreaking loss took place in the 1992 playoffs. The 10–6 Oilers traveled to Buffalo to face the Bills in the first round. Moon and the Oilers exploded from the gate, jumping to a 35–3 lead by early in the third quarter. But the Bills fought back, combining quick-strike touchdown passes with daring onside kicks. In the greatest comeback in NFL playoff history, the Bills tied the game at 38–38, forcing overtime. Minutes later, Buffalo booted a field goal to seal Houston's collapse.

THE TITANS LIGHT A FIRE

X A Heisman Trophy winner with the powerhouse Ohio State University Buckeyes, Eddie George used his speed, power, and superb stiff-arm move to become the next great Oilers rusher.

To the dismay of Houston fans, the Oilers traded Moon to the Minnesota Vikings in 1994, and in the midst of the team's first losing season in eight years, Coach Pardee was fired. Defensive coordinator Jeff Fisher was promoted to head coach, and he quickly began rebuilding the roster. Under Fisher's watch, Houston drafted quarterback Steve "Air" McNair in 1995 and running back Eddie George the following year. Together, the duo would become the heart of the team's offense. McNair was tough and versatile, equally adept at launching long bombs or scrambling for a first down. George, who would earn NFL Rookie of the Year honors in 1996, was a bruising runner who would never miss a start due to injury in his career with the club.

In addition to these roster changes, the Oilers made a geographic change as well. In 1995, Adams, who had long wanted a new stadium for his team but received little support for it in Houston, announced his intention to move the Oilers to Tennessee in 1997. While a new stadium was under construction in Nashville, the Oilers played in the Liberty Bowl in Memphis for a year and then moved to Vanderbilt Stadium in Nashville for a season. During both of these transitional years, the Oilers went a mediocre 8–8. Meanwhile, Tennessee fans clamored for a new team name that better reflected

BRUCE MATTHEWS

GUARD, OFFENSIVE TACKLE, CENTER
OILERS/TITANS SEASONS: 1983-2001
HEIGHT: 6-FOOT-5
WEIGHT: 289 POUNDS

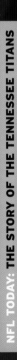

The Oilers selected Bruce Matthews in the 1983 NFL Draft, and he served them well for the next 19 seasons. "He came off the ball with such quickness, got into his blocks, great finish," said Oilers offensive lineman Mike Munchak in describing the first time he saw Matthews in training camp. "His feet were all over the place. He was like a human weed whacker." By the second game of his rookie year, Matthews had secured a starting role on the offensive line as a guard. As time passed, he showed his versatility by playing every position on the line. Despite the physical toils of his job, the durable Matthews never missed a game due to injury. He was named to 14 consecutive Pro Bowls, tying Los Angeles Rams defensive tackle Merlin Olsen for the most in NFL history. By the time he retired, Matthews had competed in 296 games, which, at that time, was more than any non-kicker in league history. In fact, his career spanned so many years that his former college teammate, Jeff Fisher, became his NFL coach.

the franchise's new home. Adams listened, and in 1999, the former Oilers took the field as the Tennessee Titans.

In addition to their new name, logo, and uniforms, the Titans had a new star: defensive end Jevon Kearse, the team's top pick in the 1999 NFL Draft. Standing 6-foot-4 and weighing 260 pounds, Kearse had such rare speed and agility that he was nicknamed "The Freak." Kearse lived up to expectations, setting an NFL rookie record with 14.5 quarterback sacks in 1999. McNair, meanwhile, led a powerful offense. George rushed for 1,304 yards in 1999, and

X Even though he remained a nightmare for quarterbacks for a number of years, Jevon Kearse would never duplicate his amazing rookie season.

safety Blaine Bishop and cornerback Samari Rolle headed up a tough defense. The Titans finished the regular season 13–3, going unbeaten at their home stadium, Adelphia Coliseum.

Tennessee continued to roll through the playoffs. The Titans won their first playoff game against the Bills with an unbelievable kickoff return in the final seconds of the game. Tennessee followed the "Music City Miracle" by fighting past the Indianapolis Colts and the Jacksonville Jaguars to reach the Super Bowl for the first time in franchise history. In a matchup against the high-scoring St. Louis Rams, the Titans came back from a 16–0 deficit to tie the game. After the Rams took a 23–16 lead with 1 minute and 54 seconds left on the clock, McNair drove the Titans down the field. Sadly, they were stopped just short of a chance at victory when Tennessee receiver Kevin Dyson was pulled down one yard shy of the end zone as time expired. "I thought it was a touchdown," said McNair. "But you have great athletes on both sides of the ball, and they made the play."

In the four seasons after their Super Bowl appearance, the Titans remained one of the elite teams of the NFL, though they could not get back to the big game. Led by McNair's strong arm and tough-as-nails leadership, as well as George's relentless rushing, Tennessee made the playoffs in 2000,

THE EIGHTH WORLD WONDER

Originally called the Harris County Domed Stadium, the Houston Astrodome was built in 1965 to accommodate both baseball and football. The first domed stadium in professional sports, the facility boasted cushioned, theater-style seats, futuristic sky boxes, and a $2-million scoreboard. Major League Baseball's Houston Astros began using the stadium—dubbed the "Eighth Wonder of the World"—in 1965, and the Oilers moved in three years later. Semi-transparent panels on the roof originally allowed natural grass to grow inside the stadium, but baseball players often complained that they could not see fly balls against the cream-colored panels. So stadium officials painted the tiles darker colors, killing the grass. To compensate, plastic grass called AstroTurf was installed to cover the stadium floor. The Astrodome seated roughly 50,000 fans, and the dome was known as a loud football stadium, making it difficult for opposing teams to hear play calls. After the 1996 season, the Oilers said goodbye to the Astrodome when they relocated to Tennessee, and the Astros left the dome in 2000. Today, the Astrodome stands largely vacant, hosting only an occasional business convention or softball game.

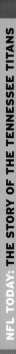

MEET THE OILERS/TITANS

JEFF FISHER

COACH
OILERS/TITANS SEASONS:
1994–PRESENT

In the early 1980s, Jeff Fisher played as a defensive back and kick-return specialist for the Chicago Bears. After an ankle injury ended his NFL playing career in 1985, he turned to coaching. By 1988, he was the Philadelphia Eagles' defensive coordinator, the youngest in the NFL. He joined the Houston Oilers as defensive coordinator in 1994 and earned the head coaching job later that year. His defensive background shaped his coaching philosophy. With the Titans, Fisher built solid rushing defenses and strong running games, encouraging his players to stay poised in times of adversity. He also showed the ability to take the team from a disappointing start to a promising finish, leading the Titans from a 1–4 start to an 11–5 finish in 2002. By 2005, he owned the team record for wins by a head coach, and by 2008, he had coached more than 200 regular-season games for the franchise. Despite staying in one job for so long, Fisher kept his outlook fresh each season. "It's like every year is my first year," he said in 2007. "I really look forward to coming to work."

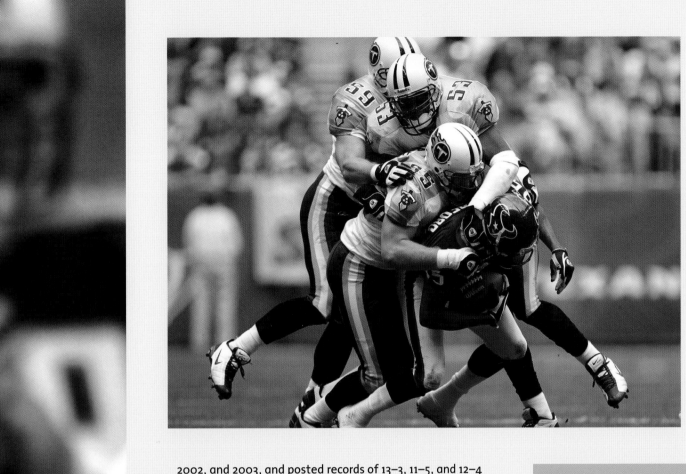

2002, and 2003, and posted records of 13–3, 11–5, and 12–4 during those years.

The 2003 season was particularly rewarding for McNair. In one game against the new Houston Texans team, McNair played with a limp from a cracked bone spur in one leg and a sore calf in the other, but he led the Titans down the field in the final minutes of the game and connected with receiver Drew Bennett for the winning score. In the playoffs, the Titans beat the Baltimore Ravens 20–17 before losing to the New England Patriots in a frigid matchup. After the season, McNair was named the NFL's co-MVP, along with Colts quarterback Peyton Manning.

X In 2002, Houston's former team met Houston's new team for the first time when the Titans clashed with the Texans and won, 17–10.

Unfortunately, that season signaled the end of an era in Tennessee, as the Titans went into rebuilding mode and began clearing out veterans to make way for younger players. The Titans released George in 2004, and two seasons after that, they traded McNair to the Ravens after selecting quarterback Vince Young with the third overall pick in the 2006 NFL Draft. "We're a scrappy, young team, definitely

✗ Vince Young came into the NFL as one of the greatest running quarterbacks in college football history, having rushed for 200 yards in his final, national title-winning game.

✗ Drew Bennett helped power the Titans' air attack in 2004, posting career bests with 1,247 receiving yards and 11 touchdowns.

X Fast linebacker Keith Bulluck helped the Titans put points on the board by returning fumbles for touchdowns in 2002, 2003, and 2006.

one of the future teams in the NFL," Titans linebacker Keith Bulluck said.

At 6-foot-5 and fast on his feet, Young was a bigger version of McNair, and he quickly became Tennessee's starter in his first season. The rookie wasted no time in showing a knack for leading his team to comeback victories. In a November 2006 game against the New York Giants, the Titans trailed 21–0 after three quarters. Young then orchestrated the biggest fourth-quarter rally in the club's history. After hitting tight end Bo Scaife on a four-yard touchdown pass, Young ran the ball himself for a score and then tossed another touchdown—this time to Brandon Jones—with 23 seconds on the clock. The Titans defense

THE MUSIC CITY MIRACLE

The "Music City Miracle" unfolded during an opening-round playoff game between the Titans and the Buffalo Bills in January 2000. The Bills kicked a field goal with 16 seconds left, moving ahead 16–15 and needing only to kick off and keep the Titans from scoring. Titans running back Lorenzo Neal received the kick and handed it off to tight end Frank Wycheck. Wycheck then drifted right before stopping and passing the ball across the field to wide receiver Kevin Dyson, who then ran 75 yards down the sidelines to score the game-winning touchdown as the Titans' Adelphia Coliseum crowd went crazy. The play, called "Home Run Throwback," was the idea of Titans special-teams coach Alan Lowry. Incredibly, Dyson had replaced an injured teammate for the kick return. Titans coach Jeff Fisher was still explaining the trick play as Dyson ran onto the field. "It was like being a little kid again, drawing something up in the dirt and then going out and doing it," Wycheck said. Bills coach Wade Phillips challenged the legality of the lateral pass, but replays showed the pass was indeed sideways, and the "miracle" was upheld.

X Sure-handed tight end Bo Scaife and quarterback Vince Young were teammates at the University of Texas before being reunited in Tennessee.

ON THE SIDELINES

BIRONAS GETS HIS KICKS

Booting 35 field goals in 2007, Titans kicker Rob Bironas not only led the league in field goals, but he also led his team in scoring. With 133 points on the season, Bironas brought consistency to every game. Before his career with the Titans, he spent time in training camp with the Green Bay Packers, Tampa Bay Buccaneers, and Pittsburgh Steelers, while also playing Arena League Football. After he found a home with the Titans in 2005, his long, accurate, last-second field goals determined the game for the Titans on more than one occasion. With a usual field-goal range of about 54 yards, he made history in December 2006, when his game-winning field goal against the Indianapolis Colts soared 60 yards to pass through the goalposts. In doing so, Bironas became only the sixth kicker in NFL history to successfully score a field goal from 60 yards or farther. He revisited the league history books in 2007, when he connected on a record eight field goals in a Titans win over the Houston Texans. "We'd rather have touchdowns," said Titans running back Chris Brown, "but we know when he goes out, it's good."

then made an interception, and with six seconds left in
regulation, kicker Rob Bironas nailed a 49-yard, game-
winning field goal to stun the Giants. At season's end, Young
was named to the Pro Bowl, making him the first rookie
quarterback since Miami Dolphins great Dan Marino in 1983
to receive the honor.

In 2007, big defensive tackle Albert Haynesworth emerged
as Tennessee's newest defensive standout. And with young
running back LenDale White pounding out 1,110 yards on the
ground, the Titans fought their way to a 10–6 record, good
enough for a playoff spot. Although they promptly lost to the

X Albert
Haynesworth was a
defensive beast in
2007, often single-
handedly collapsing
the opposing team's
offensive line.

STEVE McNAIR

QUARTERBACK
OILERS/TITANS SEASONS: 1995-2005
HEIGHT: 6-FOOT-2
WEIGHT: 230 POUNDS

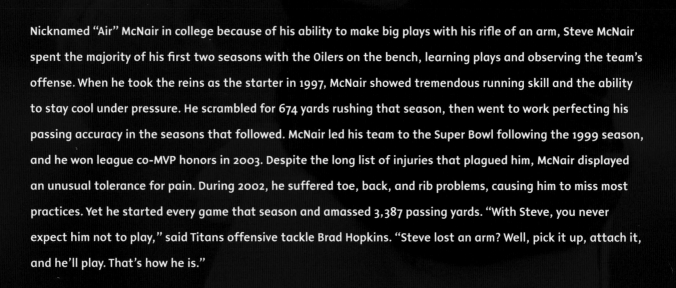

Nicknamed "Air" McNair in college because of his ability to make big plays with his rifle of an arm, Steve McNair spent the majority of his first two seasons with the Oilers on the bench, learning plays and observing the team's offense. When he took the reins as the starter in 1997, McNair showed tremendous running skill and the ability to stay cool under pressure. He scrambled for 674 yards rushing that season, then went to work perfecting his passing accuracy in the seasons that followed. McNair led his team to the Super Bowl following the 1999 season, and he won league co-MVP honors in 2003. Despite the long list of injuries that plagued him, McNair displayed an unusual tolerance for pain. During 2002, he suffered toe, back, and rib problems, causing him to miss most practices. Yet he started every game that season and amassed 3,387 passing yards. "With Steve, you never expect him not to play," said Titans offensive tackle Brad Hopkins. "Steve lost an arm? Well, pick it up, attach it, and he'll play. That's how he is."

San Diego Chargers, 17–6, the off-season addition of rookie running back Chris Johnson made them even stronger.

The Titans were one of the biggest stories in the NFL in 2008, as they started the season 10–0 behind veteran quarterback Kerry Collins (who was named the starter after Young was injured), finished the year 13–3 to secure a playoff bye and home-field advantage in the postseason. Unfortunately, despite outplaying the Baltimore Ravens in a second-round matchup, the Titans turned the ball over three times, losing 13–10 and ending an otherwise superb season on a sour note.

Since their gloriously successful start as the Oilers, the Titans franchise has featured its share of stars and memorable seasons, but the Super Bowl has always remained just beyond its grasp. But as a new generation of heroes in blue now takes the field in Tennessee, the Titans plan to finally capture the coveted Lombardi Trophy and really give the Music City something to sing about.

INDEX